US ERROR COINS GUIDE 2026

RUGH CARVER

GRAPEVINE BOOKS

Published by

GRAPEVINE BOOKS

www.grapevinebooks.com

email: contact@grapevinebooks.com

Ordering Information:

Quantity sales: Special discounts are available on quantity purchases by corporations, associations, and others.

For details, reach out to the publisher.

First published by Grapevine Books, 2025

Contents

Get Your Free E-book

Get Your Free E-book
Scan the QR code below to instantly access the e-book
'The History of Coin Minting Errors', absolutely free

SCAN ME

https://bonus.grapevinebooks.com/history-of-coin-minting-errors

INTRODUCTION
Why Coin Collecting Still Matters

You might think coin collecting is a hobby of the past, something your grandfather did with old mason jars and dusty albums. But now, the world of coins is more alive than ever. With digital currencies on the rise and physical cash slowly disappearing from daily life, coins have taken on a new kind of value. They're no longer just money. They're miniature pieces of history, stories in your palm, and sometimes, tiny mistakes that can be worth thousands of dollars.

Coin collecting, especially the hunt for error coins, blends history, strategy, and a bit of luck. Whether you're combing through your change at the coffee shop or buying rolls from the bank, every coin you touch has the potential to be a hidden treasure. With the right knowledge, even beginners can find valuable errors in circulation. That makes coin collecting not only fascinating but surprisingly rewarding.

Importance of Mint Errors in Numismatics

Numismatics, the study of money and its history, covers coins, paper currency, tokens, and medals. Within this field, error coins hold a special place. These are not just production mistakes. They are moments where the mechanical process of minting slipped, and something unique was born.

Mint errors are fascinating because they challenge the perfection of official currency. While the U.S. Mint follows strict quality control, mistakes still happen. And when they do, collectors take notice. A coin that has been struck twice, or one that has a missing part, suddenly becomes more than its face value. It becomes rare, and in the world of numismatics, rarity often means value.

Collectors love mint errors because no two are exactly alike. Even common types of errors, like off-center strikes or die cracks, can have dramatic differences from coin to coin. These differences create endless possibilities for collectors. Some people focus solely on error coins, turning a simple interest into a lifelong passion.

Brief History of Error Coins in US Minting

Mint errors have existed since the earliest days of American coinage. In the 1700s and 1800s, minting was a more manual process. This meant more room for human error, and as a result, early U.S. coins often have fascinating quirks. Misaligned dies, double strikes, and even completely wrong planchets made their way into circulation.

As minting technology improved, the number of mistakes decreased, but they never disappeared entirely. Machines still break, dies still wear out, and planchets still get misfed into presses. In fact, modern high-speed production lines, while efficient, can create new and unexpected types of errors.

Famous examples from the past include the 1955 Doubled Die Lincoln Cent and the 1943 copper penny. Both were the result of production mistakes, and both are now considered legendary among collectors. These coins remind us that even the most ordinary object, a penny, can become extraordinary when something unusual happens during minting.

In recent decades, the U.S. Mint has increased quality control, but even that hasn't eliminated all errors. In fact, some of the most desirable error coins today are relatively modern, such as certain state quarters, American Silver Eagles, and Presidential dollars. That means collectors in 2025 still have a real chance to find valuable mint errors in circulation.

What's My Coin Worth? How to Appraise & Value

One of the most common questions people ask when they find a strange-looking coin is simple: "Is this worth anything?" And the answer often depends on two things: **rarity and demand**.

Just because a coin looks unusual doesn't mean it's valuable. Some damage happens after a coin leaves the Mint, and that kind of damage does not increase a coin's value. But if the mistake happened during the minting process, and it's a documented type of error, the coin could be worth more than you think.

To appraise a coin, you'll need to identify the type of error, check the condition, and research similar sales. Online databases, auction records, and certified coin price guides like the Red Book or PCGS and NGC resources can be very helpful. But remember, price guides are just that, guides. Actual value often depends on what collectors are willing to pay at that moment.

Grading also plays a big role in value. A mint error in poor condition might not be worth much, but the same error in pristine condition could fetch a high price. That's why proper handling and storage are important. Even if you're just starting out, using gloves, coin flips, and basic magnification tools can help preserve your finds.

In this guide, you'll learn not only how to recognize valuable mint errors but also how to judge what they're worth. Whether you're holding a misstruck dime or a clipped planchet nickel, this book will walk you through the steps to become a smart, confident collector.

Welcome to the hobby. Or perhaps, the hunt. Let's begin.

SECTION 1: GETTING STARTED

1. Coin Collecting for Beginners

So you've found a strange-looking coin in your pocket change, or maybe you've heard stories about pennies worth hundreds of dollars. Welcome to the world of coin collecting, where curiosity can lead to discovery and a little bit of luck might turn spare change into treasure.

Coin collecting, also called numismatics, is more than a hobby. It's a way to learn history, spot patterns, and even invest in items that may grow in value over time. For beginners, getting started can feel overwhelming. But the truth is, you don't need to spend much, or anything at all, to begin.

Start with what you already have. Check your change jar, your wallet, your drawers. Look closely at every coin. You're not just looking for old coins. You're looking for errors, oddities, and details that stand out. Sometimes, the most valuable coins are the ones that look "wrong." Maybe the image is off-center. Maybe a number is missing. These are minting mistakes, and collectors pay serious attention to them.

Once you have a few interesting coins, the next step is learning to sort and protect them. A magnifying glass, soft cotton gloves, and basic coin holders will do. Never clean your coins. Cleaning can damage them and lower their value.

Even if a coin looks dirty or worn, it's better to leave it untouched.

Focus on U.S. coins like pennies, nickels, dimes, quarters, and half dollars. Many valuable error coins still exist in circulation. For example, some Lincoln cents have doubled letters or extra shapes near the date. Some state quarters were struck on the wrong planchet or have parts of the design missing.

Keep a notebook or use a free app to track your finds. Record dates, mint marks, errors, and conditions. Join a local coin club or online forum. You'll learn faster by sharing what you find.

You don't need to be an expert to enjoy this hobby. Just sharp eyes, a little patience, and curiosity. Most importantly, have fun. Every coin has a story. Some tell of history. Others tell of mistakes. And some might just change your life.

2. Understanding Pocket Change Treasures

Millions of coins pass through people's hands every day, unnoticed. But among that change could be a coin that's worth far more than its face value. These are pocket change treasures, and they're still out there.

It's not always about age. Older coins can be common and worn. The real treasures are mint errors, coins made incorrectly at the U.S. Mint. These include doubled images, off-center strikes, die cracks, clipped planchets, and more.

Take a close look at your coins. Are the letters blurry or doubled? Is something missing? These small flaws could make a coin worth several dollars, or even hundreds.

And you pay nothing to find them. Some of the most famous error coins were discovered in grocery store change or bank rolls. A 1995 Lincoln cent with a doubled die obverse can be worth $20 or more.

Recent coins are still worth checking. Even with modern minting standards, mistakes slip through. State quarters, Presidential dollars, and modern nickels all have known errors still in circulation.

Keep a jar or container just for odd coins. Review them later with a magnifier and good light. Use reference guides and check online communities if you're unsure.

Even if some coins turn out to be post-mint damage, you'll still be learning. And every once in a while, you'll come across something truly special.

3. Coin Collector Supplies You Actually Need

You don't need fancy equipment to start collecting coins. Most beginners only need a few simple tools.

Start with a **magnifying glass**. This helps you see tiny details like doubling or repunched mint marks. A 5x to 10x handheld magnifier works fine.

Use **cotton gloves** to handle coins, especially uncirculated or shiny ones. Finger oils can stain or damage them. Always hold coins by the edges.

Store your coins in **holders or flips**. These keep your coins safe and allow for easy labeling. Avoid cheap plastic holders with PVC.

A **coin album or storage box** helps as your collection grows. You can sort by type, error, or date.

Good lighting matters. Natural light is best, but a bright lamp works too. View coins from multiple angles to catch hidden flaws.

Keep a **notebook or digital tracker** to log your finds. This builds your knowledge and helps you spot trends.

Finally, get a **reliable guidebook**, like the Red Book or a specialized error coin reference. It helps you identify and understand what you're seeing.

With these tools, you can care for and expand your collection without spending much.

4. Coin Roll Hunting Finds and How to Do It Right

Coin roll hunting means getting rolls of coins from banks and searching through them for errors, silver coins, or rare dates. It's one of the most fun and cost-effective ways to collect.

Start by visiting your local bank. Ask for rolls of coins, pennies, nickels, dimes, or quarters. Some banks may be more helpful than others, so build good relationships with the staff.

Open your rolls carefully and inspect each coin. Look for doubling, clipped planchets, die cracks, or anything that looks strange. Older dates and silver content are also worth checking for.

Use your magnifier and good lighting. Even small details can mean big value. Compare anything unusual to trusted guides.

Sort coins as you go. Make separate piles for potential errors, coins worth saving, and regular ones to return.

As you gain confidence, you might want to request full boxes of coins. More coins mean more chances to find something special.

Track your results to identify patterns. Maybe one bank gives you older coins. Maybe you spot a certain date showing up often. These notes can guide future hunts.

Be respectful. Banks are not required to give out coin rolls. Return unused coins neatly. Some collectors even open business accounts to make things smoother.

Coin roll hunting is part treasure hunt, part detective work. It costs almost nothing, but it offers knowledge, excitement, and the real possibility of finding a valuable piece of minting history.

SECTION 2:
WHAT ARE ERROR COINS?

5. What Qualifies as a Mint Error?

Not every strange-looking coin is a mint error. Some are damaged after they leave the U.S. Mint, while others simply show signs of circulation. A true mint error is a mistake that occurs during the minting process itself before the coin ever enters public hands.

Mint errors fall into three main categories: **planchet preparation errors**, **die creation errors**, and **striking errors**.

Planchet Errors

The **planchet** is the blank metal disc before it's stamped with a design. If a coin is struck on a faulty planchet, it becomes a mint error. One common example is a **clipped planchet**, where part of the coin appears cut off. Another is a **lamination error**, where metal peels or flakes due to poor bonding or contamination. These mistakes are made before striking and are fully legitimate errors.

Die Errors

The **die** is the metal tool that presses the coin's design onto the planchet. When a die is flawed, every coin it strikes carries the same mistake. A famous example is the **doubled die**, where parts of the design appear to be doubled. The 1955 Lincoln cent is the best-known example.

Other die errors include the **repunched mint mark**, where the mint mark was punched into the die more than once, and **die cracks** or **cuds**, caused by damaged or broken dies. These result in raised lines or blobs on the finished coin.

Striking Errors

Striking errors happen when the coin is pressed between the dies. An **off-center strike** occurs when the planchet is misaligned, leaving part of the design missing. A **broadstrike** happens when the collar that shapes the coin fails, resulting in a coin that is wider and flatter than usual.

Other rare examples include **multiple strikes** and **mule errors**, where dies from two different coin types are mistakenly used together. Mule coins are extremely rare and valuable.

What Doesn't Count

Damage caused by heat, chemicals, machines, or handling after the mint does not count as a mint error. Coins with scratches, stains, or discoloration are considered damaged, not collectible mistakes.

Final Tip

If the flaw happened inside the mint, it may be valuable. If it happened outside, it's just damage. Knowing this difference is the first step in becoming a smart collector.

6. Difference Between Errors, Varieties, and Counterfeits

In coin collecting, not every odd-looking coin is what it seems. Some coins are genuine mint errors, others are intentional design varieties, and a few are outright fakes. Understanding the difference between these three categories is essential if you want to become a skilled and confident collector.

Let's break each one down clearly and then compare them side by side.

What Are Mint Errors?

Mint errors are unintentional mistakes made during the production of coins at the United States Mint. These mistakes occur during one of the three major stages of the minting process: planchet preparation, die creation, or striking.

These mistakes are often unique and unpredictable. Their value depends on how dramatic the error is, how rare it is, and how visible the problem appears on the coin. The key is that the mint did not intend for these flaws to happen.

What Are Varieties?

Varieties are intentional design differences or repeated changes that occur during the minting process. Unlike errors, varieties are not accidents. They are usually the result of planned modifications, differences between dies, or changes in engraving.

Varieties are typically consistent across many coins, meaning that the same variety appears repeatedly. Collectors often seek them out because they are cataloged, recognized by grading services, and can carry strong historical interest.

What Are Counterfeits?

Counterfeit coins are not made by the U.S. Mint at all. These are fake coins created by individuals trying to deceive others for profit. Some counterfeits are crude and easy to spot. Others are skillfully made and require expertise to identify.

Counterfeits are illegal to sell as authentic coins. Learning how to spot them is critical for protecting yourself and your collection.

Comparison Table: Errors vs Varieties vs Counterfeits

Feature	Mint Error Coin	Variety Coin	Counterfeit Coin
Origin	U.S. Mint accident	U.S. Mint intentional variation	Made outside the U.S. Mint

Feature	Mint Error Coin	Variety Coin	Counterfeit Coin
Repetition	Random, usually one-of-a-kind	Repeated across many coins	Replicated to deceive
Intention	Not intentional	Intentional design difference	Intentionally fake
Value to Collectors	Often high if visible and rare	Often high, especially famous varieties	No legitimate collector value
Authentication Needed	Often helpful, especially for dramatic ones	Frequently verified by grading services	Always should be checked or avoided
Examples	Off-center, die crack, broadstrike	Doubled die, repunched mint mark, Wide AM	1943 copper penny copy, fake Morgan dollar
Legality	Legal to own and sell	Legal to own and sell	Illegal to sell as genuine
Grading Services Accept?	Yes	Yes	No, unless marked "copy" or novelty

Why It Matters

Understanding the difference between these three categories helps you avoid mistakes when buying or selling coins. Many new collectors see a damaged or strange-looking coin and believe it is a valuable error. In reality, it might just be post-mint damage or even a fake. By learning the characteristics of genuine errors and varieties, you protect your collection and make smarter decisions.

For example, if you find a coin with a doubled design, that might sound like a mint error. But not all doubled designs are true doubled dies. Some are machine doubling, a common form of mechanical shift that looks similar but has no added value. A true doubled die comes from a flaw in the die itself, making it a variety. Knowing that distinction can mean the difference between a coin worth 10 cents and one worth 100 dollars.

Similarly, some fake coins are made to resemble real ones, but with closer inspection you'll notice blurry details, unusual weight, or strange color. A simple magnet test, scale, or reference check against official mint specifications can quickly rule out a counterfeit.

Final Advice

If you're ever unsure whether a coin is an error, a variety, or a counterfeit, seek a second opinion. Use resources like online collector forums, trusted dealers, or third-party grading services. Many professional graders are trained to spot fakes and identify legitimate mint issues. Their expertise can give you peace of mind and help you avoid costly mistakes.

By mastering the differences between these three categories, you'll build confidence, avoid being fooled, and develop a collector's eye for spotting value where others see ordinary change.

7. Identifying Mint Mistakes in Circulation

The thrill of coin collecting often begins with a simple discovery. A coin that looks a little off. Maybe the rim is too wide on one side, or the letters appear slightly crooked. These subtle oddities may be signs of mint mistakes, errors made during the coin's production at the U.S. Mint that ended up in circulation.

Many valuable mint errors are still out there, hidden in pocket change, bank rolls, or even tip jars. With practice and the right tools, you can learn to spot these overlooked treasures.

How to Begin

Start by slowing down and observing your coins. Most people handle coins without ever examining them. A collector, however, treats each coin like a potential find. Use a magnifying glass with 5x to 10x magnification and examine your coins under bright light. Sometimes, a slight tilt or shift in angle is all it takes to reveal an error.

Where to Look

Pay close attention to these areas:

- **Date and mint mark**: Look for doubling, odd spacing, or repunching.
- **Edges and rims**: Check for unusual thickness, missing sections, or incomplete rims.
- **Lettering**: Search for letters that are doubled, distorted, or cracked.
- **Main design**: Examine for shifted images, rotated elements, or missing parts.
- **Surface**: Look for signs of peeling, flaking, or rough patches that might indicate lamination errors.

Common Mint Errors You Can Find

1. **Off-center strikes**: These coins are not struck in the correct position. The more off-center the design, the more valuable the coin, especially if the date is still visible.
2. **Clipped planchets**: Coins that appear to have a small piece missing along the edge due to poor cutting.
3. **Doubled die errors**: These coins show doubling on numbers, letters, or design features. The 1972 and 1995 Lincoln cents are classic examples.

4. **Die cracks and cuds**: Raised lines or blobs near the rim signal a worn or broken die.
5. **Lamination flaws**: Peeling or flaking metal caused by impurities in the planchet.
6. **Repunched mint marks**: Visible doubling of the mint mark due to misaligned punches.
7. **Broadstrikes**: Coins that appear wider and flatter due to missing retaining collars during striking.

Helpful Tools

A digital scale, calipers, and updated error coin guides can help confirm your suspicions. Online collector forums also offer feedback and support from experienced hobbyists.

Avoiding False Errors

Coins altered by heat, chemicals, or damage after leaving the mint may look strange but are not true mint errors. Compare suspicious coins to normal examples of the same year and mint. If the difference came from the minting process, it's likely real.

Final Tip

Keep a small "question pile" for coins you're unsure about. Review them later with fresh eyes or post photos online for advice. With curiosity and consistency, even spare change can reveal remarkable surprises.

8. Tools for Identifying Errors in Your Pocket

You don't need a high-tech laboratory to start finding error coins. With just a few basic tools and a sharp eye, you can begin identifying mint mistakes in your own pocket change. These tools are affordable, easy to use, and perfect for beginners and experienced collectors alike.

Magnifying Glass or Loupe

The most important tool for spotting small errors is a **magnifier**. A 5x to 10x handheld magnifying glass or jeweler's loupe is perfect for revealing tiny details like doubling, die cracks, or repunched mint marks. Choose one with clear glass and good lighting support, such as a built-in LED.

Good Lighting

Lighting is just as important as magnification. A **bright desk lamp** or natural sunlight allows you to see the coin's surface clearly. Shadows and glare can hide subtle errors, so try tilting the coin at different angles under the light.

Digital Scale

Some mint errors cause coins to weigh more or less than they should. A **digital scale** that measures in grams to two decimal places can help you detect underweight or overweight coins, which may signal planchet issues or missing details.

Calipers or Ruler

Use **digital calipers** or a simple ruler to measure the coin's diameter and thickness. Errors like broadstrikes or overstruck coins may not match standard measurements.

Reference Books and Apps

Having a reliable **coin guidebook** nearby is essential. The Red Book, Cherrypickers' Guide, or error coin-specific references provide images and descriptions to compare your finds. Mobile apps and online catalogs are also great for quick checks.

Containers and Notebooks

Use small trays or flips to separate suspicious coins from regular change. A **notebook** or spreadsheet can help you track dates, mint marks, and notes about the condition or suspected error.

With these tools, your loose change becomes a mini treasure hunt. By observing closely and staying organized, you'll build confidence and develop the skills needed to spot genuine mint mistakes hiding in plain sight.

SECTION 3: TYPES OF MINT ERRORS

9. Die Errors: Doubled Die Obverse, Die Cracks, Cuds, and Die Clash

Die errors occur during the creation or deterioration of the dies used to stamp coins. The die is the engraved metal piece that strikes a coin's design onto a blank planchet. When the die is flawed, every coin it strikes can carry that same mistake. These are among the most sought-after and recognizable mint errors in numismatics.

Doubled Die Obverse

One of the most famous and collectible die errors is the **doubled die obverse**, often shortened to DDO. This error happens during the creation of the die itself. In the early stages of die production, a working die receives multiple impressions from a hub. If the die shifts between these impressions, it results in a doubled image. Every coin struck by this flawed die shows the same doubling.

The most famous example is the **1955 Lincoln cent**, where the date and lettering are clearly doubled and visible without magnification. Other well-known years include the 1972 and 1995 Lincoln cents. Doubling is typically seen on the date, mint mark, and inscriptions like "LIBERTY" or "IN GOD WE TRUST."

It is important not to confuse true doubled die coins with **machine doubling**, which results from loose machinery and causes a flatter, shelf-like doubling. Machine doubling does not add collector value, while true doubled die coins can be worth hundreds or even thousands of dollars.

Die Cracks

Over time, dies experience stress and wear, especially after striking thousands of coins. This wear can lead to small fractures in the die surface. When this cracked die strikes a planchet, it leaves a raised line on the coin. These are called **die cracks** and can range from tiny hairline marks to long cracks running across the coin.

While minor die cracks may not carry much premium, more dramatic or unusual die cracks can increase a coin's interest and value, especially when they create distinctive patterns or run through major parts of the design.

Cuds

A **cud** is a specific kind of die break. It occurs when a part of the die near the edge of the coin breaks off completely. When this damaged die strikes a planchet, the area where the die is missing fills with metal. On the coin, it appears as a solid, raised blob near the rim, sometimes obliterating part of the design or lettering.

Cuds can vary in size and shape. Some collectors specialize in cud errors and assign nicknames to especially unique or dramatic examples. Unlike die chips or cracks, cuds are larger and generally more valued.

Die Clash

A **die clash** happens when the obverse and reverse dies strike each other without a planchet between them. This can occur due to a mechanical error or misfeed in the striking process. When the dies hit each other directly, they leave behind parts of their designs on each other's surface.

As a result, subsequent coins struck by the damaged dies may show ghost-like images of the opposite design in areas where they should not appear. For example, you might see part of the reverse design faintly on the obverse side. Die clash marks are subtle but fascinating, and many collectors find them highly appealing, especially when the clashed design is clearly visible.

10. Planchet Errors: Clipped Planchet and Lamination Error

Planchet errors happen before a coin is struck. These flaws originate during the preparation of the blank metal discs that eventually become coins. While planchet errors can be small, they often produce visually striking results.

Clipped Planchet

One of the easiest planchet errors to identify is the **clipped planchet**. This occurs when the metal strip used to punch out blank discs is not properly aligned, causing the punch to overlap an existing hole. The result is a blank planchet with a curved or straight piece missing from the edge.

The clipped section typically shows smooth edges and may even display a "Blakesley effect," which is a weakly struck rim opposite the clip due to uneven pressure during the strike. If the design is centered well and the clip does not remove key features like the date or mint mark, the coin can still be highly collectible.

Straight clips, ragged clips, and curved clips are all variations of this error. The more dramatic the missing piece, the higher the value, especially if the coin is in good condition and clearly shows the minting flaw.

Lamination Error

A **lamination error** is a problem within the planchet's metal composition. It usually occurs when impurities or improper bonding affect the integrity of the metal. When the coin is struck, parts of the surface can peel, flake, or split.

These errors appear as jagged, raised patches or thin, curling pieces that seem to be peeling off the coin. In some cases, a piece of the metal completely separates from the coin, leaving a void. Lamination errors can affect one or both sides and often vary in size and appearance.

While not always highly valuable, lamination errors are interesting to collectors because they reveal problems at the earliest stage of production. They also have a rugged, natural look that makes them visually distinct.

11. Striking Errors: Off-Center Strike and Broadstrike

Striking errors occur at the final stage of coin production, when the prepared planchet is pressed between the obverse and reverse dies. If something goes wrong during this step, the resulting coin can look very unusual and may be worth much more than its face value.

Off-Center Strike

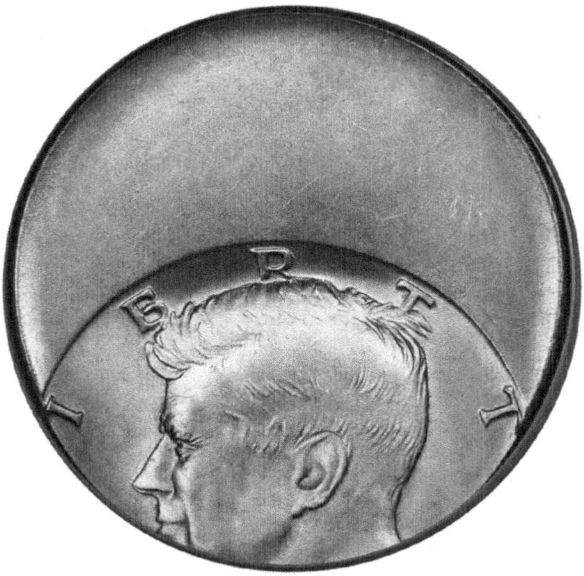

An **off-center strike** happens when the planchet is not correctly seated between the dies. When struck, the coin ends up with part of its design missing, and a blank crescent or curve appears along the edge.

The value of an off-center coin depends on how far the strike is off and whether key features like the date and mint mark are still visible. A coin that is ten percent off-center may have only a small blank area, while one that is eighty percent off-center might have almost no design at all.

Collectors especially seek off-center coins that are dramatically misaligned but still show the full date. These coins offer a clear and exciting example of a mint mistake and often command a premium price.

Broadstrike

A **broadstrike** occurs when the collar die, the circular retaining ring that shapes the edge of the coin, is missing or malfunctioning. Without this collar, the metal flows outward during the strike, producing a coin that is wider and flatter than usual. It lacks the raised rim found on normal coins and may appear slightly warped.

Despite the unusual shape, the coin still has a complete design, and its diameter is usually larger than standard. Broadstrikes can happen on any denomination and are relatively easy to recognize.

Unlike off-center strikes, broadstrikes preserve the central design. That makes them a fascinating example of a mechanical failure without losing the core image of the coin. They are especially prized when they occur on larger coins, such as half dollars or dollar coins.

12. Mule Error Coins and Other Extreme Mistakes

Most mint errors are subtle. A slight off-center strike or a small die crack may go unnoticed by the average person. But then there are **extreme mistakes**, errors so dramatic and rare that they stop collectors in their tracks. Chief among these are **mule errors**, along with striking anomalies that seem almost impossible. These coins are true outliers, and they often command high prices due to their shock value and rarity.

What Is a Mule Error Coin?

A **mule error** happens when a coin is struck using two mismatched dies, which are dies that were never meant to be paired. This might mean that the obverse (front) die is from one coin type while the reverse (back) die is from another. Since each denomination and series has specially matched dies, mixing them is a serious minting mistake.

The most famous example is the **2000 Sacagawea dollar mule**, which features the obverse of a Washington quarter and the reverse of a Sacagawea dollar. This coin should not exist. Yet somehow, it was struck and released. Only a few dozen are known to exist, and each one has sold for tens of thousands of dollars.

Mule errors are often caused by a lapse during the die installation process at the mint. Because dies are handled manually in some stages, it is possible, though rare, for the wrong die to be paired and used for striking.

Other Extreme Errors

Beyond mules, there are other wild minting mistakes that have made it into circulation. These include:

- **Double denominations**: A coin struck first with one denomination and then again with a die for another.
- **Coins struck on foreign planchets**: Sometimes blanks intended for foreign countries end up in U.S. mint presses.
- **Wrong metal compositions**: A coin may be struck on a planchet intended for a different series or year.
- **Triple strikes or extreme multiple strikes**: Coins hit multiple times in clearly separated strikes, creating ghosted or overlapping images.

These errors are extremely rare and valuable. They are almost always authenticated by grading services and often receive coverage in numismatic journals or collector news.

13. Repunched Mint Marks and Rotated Dies

Not all mint errors are as dramatic as a mule. Some are small, precise, and appreciated for their technical interest. Two well-known types in this category are **repunched mint marks (RPMs)** and **rotated dies**. These errors often require close inspection but are still very collectible.

Repunched Mint Marks (RPM)

Before the mid-1980s, mint marks were punched manually onto each working die. This meant that every die had to be aligned by hand. If the punch slipped or was misaligned, the mint mark could be punched again in a slightly different position. The result is a **repunched mint mark**, or RPM.

RPMs usually appear as shadows, doubling, or ghost images of the mint mark next to the primary one. Sometimes the extra punch is above, below, or slightly beside the main mark. While these may seem minor, they are official die characteristics and are documented by major grading services and guides.

Examples of well-known RPMs include:

- 1960-D Lincoln cent (small date over large date)
- 1956-D Jefferson nickel with strong repunching
- 1970-S Lincoln cent RPM varieties

RPMs can add significant value to a coin, especially when clearly visible and well-centered.

Rotated Dies

Normally, the front and back designs of a coin should align when the coin is flipped top to bottom. This is called **coin alignment**. However, if one of the dies is incorrectly installed or shifts during production, the reverse may appear rotated when compared to the obverse.

This type of error is called a **rotated die error**. It can range from slight misalignment to a full 180-degree rotation. While minor rotations may not increase value much, extreme rotations, such as 90 or 180 degrees, are highly desirable.

Collectors test for rotation by flipping the coin vertically. If the reverse design is upside down or tilted at an odd angle, the coin may have a rotated die error. These are especially valuable when paired with other visible errors.

14. Guide: Photos of Typical U.S. Mint Errors

Understanding mint errors becomes much easier when you know exactly what to look for. Use this reference to identify common U.S. mint errors based on visual markers. Each entry describes what to look for in photographs or under magnification.

Doubled Die Obverse (DDO)

- **Description:** Thick, shadow-like doubling on lettering or date.
- **Key Areas:** LIBERTY, IN GOD WE TRUST, date.
- **Example Dates:** 1955, 1972, 1995 Lincoln cents.
- **Identification:** Bold duplication visible to the naked eye in strong examples.

Off-Center Strike

- **Description:** Design is struck off the center of the coin, leaving a blank crescent.
- **Value Factors:** More dramatic shifts and visible date/mint mark increase value.
- **Identification:** Obvious missing portion on one side of the coin.

Clipped Planchet

- **Description:** A section of the coin's edge is missing due to a miscut during blanking.
- **Edges:** Smooth, often curved; Blakesley effect may be present on the opposite side.
- **Identification:** Bite-like chunk missing; no signs of post-mint damage.

Lamination Error

- **Description:** Peeling or flaking of metal layers due to alloy flaws.
- **Appearance:** Jagged patches or surface splits, often raised or curling.
- **Identification:** Can occur on one or both sides; resembles metal detachment.

Die Crack

- **Description:** Thin, raised lines across the surface from a cracked die.
- **Location:** Often starts from the rim and runs inward.
- **Identification:** Follows design contours; appears like a scratch but raised.

Cud

- **Description:** Raised, blob-like mass of metal at the rim.
- **Cause:** A piece of the die breaks off completely.
- **Identification:** Distorts surrounding design and lettering.

Die Clash

- **Description:** Ghost-like impressions from the opposite die.
- **Example:** Reverse design may appear faintly on the obverse.
- **Identification:** Subtle, often requires angled light to view clearly.

Broadstrike

- **Description:** Coin is struck without the retaining collar.
- **Appearance:** Flattened, wider coin with no raised rim.
- **Identification:** Full design present but rimless and stretched.

Rotated Die

- **Description:** Obverse and reverse designs are misaligned.
- **Identification Method:** Flip coin top-to-bottom; rotated reverse will not align upright.
- **Measurement:** Rotation is noted in degrees (e.g., 45°, 180°).

Mule Error

- **Description:** Obverse and reverse designs from two different coin types.
- **Example:** Washington quarter obverse with Sacagawea dollar reverse.
- **Identification:** Dramatically mismatched designs; requires certification for confirmation.

SECTION 4:
ERROR COINS BY DENOMINATION

15. Lincoln Cent Errors: DDO, BIE, and RPM

The Lincoln cent is the most widely collected coin in the United States, and for good reason. With over a century of circulation and billions of coins struck, the Lincoln cent offers a treasure trove of errors and varieties. Among the most famous and frequently collected are **doubled die obverse (DDO)** errors, **BIE varieties**, and **repunched mint marks (RPMs)**.

Doubled Die Obverse (DDO)

Perhaps the most legendary of all Lincoln cent errors is the **1955 doubled die obverse**. The doubling on this coin is so dramatic that it can be seen without magnification. The date, LIBERTY, and IN GOD WE TRUST all appear heavily shadowed and doubled. Fewer than 25,000 were released into circulation, and today, even worn examples can sell for hundreds of dollars.

Other notable Lincoln DDOs include the **1972**, **1983**, and **1995** cents. While the doubling is not as bold as the 1955 variety, these coins still attract attention and are listed in major reference books. Any coin showing signs of doubling on the obverse, especially the date and lettering, should be set aside for closer inspection.

BIE Error

The **BIE error** is a fun and accessible variety that appears in many Lincoln cents from the 1950s and 1960s. It gets its name from a small die break that forms between the B and E in the word LIBERTY, making it appear as if there's an "I" in between.

While not technically a major mint error, the BIE variety is a result of a die crack, and many collectors build full sets of BIE cents. Their value is usually modest, but they are a great entry point into die break collecting and provide insight into how dies deteriorate over time.

Repunched Mint Mark (RPM)

Before 1990, mint marks were applied to dies by hand. This manual process often led to the mint mark being punched more than once, slightly out of alignment. These are called **repunched mint marks**, or RPMs.

Well-known RPM examples in the Lincoln cent series include:

- **1956-D**, with strong repunching visible north of the main D
- **1960-D small date over large date**
- **1970-S large date RPMs**

RPMs are collectible and often listed in specialized references such as the Cherrypickers' Guide.

16. Jefferson Nickel Mistakes Worth Spotting

Introduced in 1938, the **Jefferson nickel** series is known for its design longevity and wartime silver compositions, but it also includes several intriguing errors and varieties. While less famous than the Lincoln cent errors, Jefferson nickels have hidden gems that can be found in circulation or in bulk coin lots.

Full Steps Designation

Before diving into specific errors, it's worth noting the **Full Steps** grading standard. On the reverse of the Jefferson nickel, Monticello's front steps should appear sharp and complete. Coins with five or six fully visible steps can bring a premium, even without an error. Weak strikes or die wear often obscure these details.

Doubled Dies

Though not as dramatic as those seen on cents, Jefferson nickels do have **doubled die varieties**, especially from the 1939 and 1943 issues. The **1939 DDO** shows doubling on the words MONTICELLO and FIVE CENTS. This error is highly sought after and commands strong value in higher grades.

Another key is the **1943-P war nickel** doubled die. Doubling is visible on the reverse lettering and is a popular variety among silver coin collectors.

Overdates and RPMs

In 1942, both silver and copper-nickel versions of the Jefferson nickel were struck. One of the most famous varieties is the **1942-D over horizontal D**, where the original mint mark was punched sideways and corrected. Though subtle, this overdate is valuable in good condition.

RPMs in the Jefferson series are less common but still collectible. The **1954-S RPM** and several from the early 1960s show visible repunching under magnification.

17. Roosevelt Dime Errors That Are Actually Valuable

The **Roosevelt dime**, minted since 1946, may be small in size, but it carries several important errors that have caught the attention of collectors. Dimes are often overlooked in circulation, which makes them a quiet but rewarding target for error hunting.

Silver vs Clad Composition

The most basic check for early Roosevelt dimes is their metal content. Dimes minted from 1946 to 1964 are **90 percent silver**. These are worth more than face value due to their bullion content. Even in worn condition, they are worth several dollars each.

After 1964, dimes were made with a copper-nickel clad composition. Occasionally, silver planchets remained in the mint presses after the switch. This resulted in rare **1965 dimes struck on silver planchets**. These can be identified by weight and color.

Doubled Dies

Several Roosevelt dimes feature **doubled die reverses**, especially on the torch, lettering, and flames. Notable dates include:

- **1963 DDR** with doubling on E PLURIBUS UNUM
- **1982 DDR**, one of the more dramatic modern examples

These varieties often require magnification but are cataloged and known in the collector community.

No Mint Mark Error

In 1982, a now-famous mistake occurred when the Philadelphia Mint struck dimes **without a mint mark**. Normally, dimes from Philadelphia have no mint mark, but in 1980 the mint began including a "P" on coins.

The **1982 no-P dime** is a true error, and only a small number escaped into circulation. These dimes are now highly collectible, especially in higher grades.

18. Washington Quarter Varieties and State Quarter Errors

The **Washington quarter** has been in use since 1932 and offers one of the widest ranges of mint errors, thanks in part to its long run and the introduction of new series like the **State Quarters** and **America the Beautiful** designs.

Silver Quarters

Washington quarters minted from 1932 to 1964 contain **90 percent silver**. These carry intrinsic metal value and are often pulled from circulation by savvy collectors. After 1964, quarters were struck with a copper-nickel clad composition.

Check for **1965 quarters struck on silver planchets**. These transitional errors weigh more and have no visible copper layer on the rim.

Doubled Dies

Some of the most dramatic Washington quarter errors include doubled dies. Notable examples include:

- **1934 DDO**, with doubling visible on IN GOD WE TRUST
- **1976 bicentennial quarter DDR**, with strong doubling on UNITED STATES OF AMERICA and E PLURIBUS UNUM

These errors are highly collectible and appear in major guides.

State Quarter Errors

The State Quarter Program, which ran from 1999 to 2008, introduced fifty new reverse designs. This high-output period also produced numerous mint errors and varieties.

Some highlights include:

- **2004 Wisconsin "Extra Leaf" quarters**: These show an extra piece of corn husk, known as the "high leaf" and "low leaf" varieties. Both versions are collectible and can sell for over fifty dollars each.
- **2005 Kansas "In God We Rust" error**: Caused by a filled die, the "T" in TRUST is missing, resulting in the now-famous phrase. While not a true doubled die, it is widely collected.
- **2001 New York Off-Center Strike**: Some New York quarters were found with dramatic off-center strikes, making them desirable mint errors.

Reverse Rotation Errors

In some Washington and State Quarters, the reverse appears rotated when the coin is flipped. These **rotated die errors** are measurable in degrees and can range from subtle to extreme. Coins with a 90- or 180-degree rotation are especially valuable.

19. Kennedy Half Dollar Surprises

The **Kennedy half dollar**, introduced in 1964 to honor President John F. Kennedy after his assassination, holds a unique place in U.S. coinage. Though rarely seen in day-to-day transactions today, it has produced several interesting surprises and varieties that collectors should be aware of.

90 Percent and 40 Percent Silver Coins

The first Kennedy half dollars struck in 1964 were made of **90 percent silver**. These coins were heavily hoarded and rarely circulated. From 1965 to 1970, the Mint continued producing Kennedy halves with **40 percent silver content**, making them desirable for bullion value even in worn condition.

If you come across a 1964 half dollar, you are holding one of the last high-silver circulating coins in U.S. history. The 1965 to 1970 issues also contain silver but are often overlooked due to their slightly different appearance and weight.

1970-D and 1987 Issues

Both the **1970-D** and **1987-P/D** Kennedy half dollars were not issued for general circulation. They were included only in special collector sets. Despite being relatively modern, they are considered low-mintage coins. If found in circulation, they are valuable because of their limited release and collectibility.

1974-D Doubled Die Obverse

One of the more famous Kennedy errors is the **1974-D doubled die obverse**.

The doubling is most prominent on the inscriptions IN GOD WE TRUST and LIBERTY. This variety was not widely known until the 1990s and remains an exciting find for collectors. It is worth searching for in bulk lots or rolls.

1982 No "FG" Initials

Some 1982 and 1983 Kennedy halves are missing the initials "FG" (for designer Frank Gasparro) on the reverse, near the bottom right of the eagle's tail. This occurred due to die polishing and can raise the value of the coin if it is clearly missing the initials.

Kennedy halves are rarely found in everyday transactions, but they are still produced in small numbers each year. Many banks carry them by request, making roll searching a useful strategy for spotting these overlooked treasures.

20. American Silver Eagle Varieties for Bullion Investors

The **American Silver Eagle**, first issued in 1986, is the official silver bullion coin of the United States. Containing one troy ounce of 99.9 percent pure silver, it is primarily targeted at investors, but it has also become a favorite among collectors due to its size, beauty, and the occasional production surprises.

Burnished, Proof, and Bullion Strikes

Silver Eagles come in several formats:

- **Bullion strike** coins have no mint mark and are intended for investors.
- **Proof strike** coins are struck multiple times and have a mirror-like background, typically with a "W" mint mark for West Point.
- **Burnished coins**, also called uncirculated collector versions, have a matte finish and are usually struck at West Point with a "W" mint mark as well.

Each version has different mintage levels and price points. Some collectors aim to complete full sets of each type, year by year.

1995-W Proof

One of the most famous Silver Eagles is the **1995-W proof**, which was only available as part of a gold coin set and had a very low mintage. It is widely considered the key coin in the Silver Eagle series and commands thousands of dollars in high grades.

Type 1 and Type 2 Reverse Changes

In 2021, the Silver Eagle design changed for the first time in its history. The original **Heraldic Eagle reverse** (now called Type 1) was replaced with a new **Flying Eagle reverse** (Type 2). Both versions were minted in 2021, creating a special dual-year variety.

Collectors look for differences between the two, and special designations from grading companies make them more desirable to those building complete type sets.

Minting Errors and Varieties

While the Silver Eagle is struck with great precision, a few rare **minting errors** have surfaced over the years. These include:

- Coins struck on planchets intended for other denominations
- Weak or missing edge lettering on special issues
- Strike-through errors, often from debris caught in the die

Because of their higher value, even small mistakes on Silver Eagles can attract attention. Investors and collectors alike watch closely for these outliers.

21. Valuable Coins Still in Circulation

Despite the rise of digital payments, coins are still used every day, and some of them are worth far more than face value. Here are a few key coins that may still be found in circulation or coin rolls today.

1992 Close AM Lincoln Cent

Most Lincoln cents from 1992 have a wide gap between the letters "A" and "M" in AMERICA. However, a few were struck using a reverse intended for proof coins, resulting in a **close AM**. If found in circulation, this coin can be worth hundreds, even in worn condition.

1982 Small Date Copper Cent

In 1982, the Mint transitioned from copper to zinc for Lincoln cents. That year also featured both large and small date designs. A **1982 small date struck in copper** is rare. To identify one, you'll need a precise scale. Copper cents weigh 3.11 grams, while zinc cents weigh 2.5 grams.

1972 Doubled Die Cent

Although heavily searched, the **1972 doubled die obverse Lincoln cent** can still be found. Doubling is visible on the date and lettering. Lesser-known 1972 DDO varieties exist as well and may not be immediately recognized by casual collectors.

State Quarters with Errors

The State Quarters series introduced numerous error varieties. Some of the most valuable include:

- **2004 Wisconsin Extra Leaf High and Low**
- **2005 Minnesota with extra trees**
- **2001-P New York off-center strikes**

These quarters are still in circulation and can sell for twenty to fifty dollars or more depending on condition.

1965–1970 Kennedy Half Dollars

As mentioned earlier, Kennedy half dollars from this range contain **40 percent silver**, giving them intrinsic value. Since they are still legal tender, they occasionally appear in rolls or as change from coin-counting machines.

Silver Dimes and Quarters

Any **Roosevelt dime** dated 1964 or earlier is 90 percent silver. The same applies to **Washington quarters** from 1964 or earlier. Though rare, these coins do show up in pocket change, especially when cash registers are emptied at the end of a business day.

Foreign Coins and Oddities

While not U.S. legal tender, some **Canadian and foreign coins** enter circulation unnoticed. These include older Canadian nickels and dimes with silver content or unusual designs that can interest collectors.

SECTION 5: GRADING AND CERTIFICATION

22. Coin Grading Standards Explained Simply

Coin grading is the process of evaluating a coin's condition to determine its value. Grading helps collectors understand what a coin is worth and gives them a way to compare coins across the market. While professionals use precise systems, beginners can quickly learn the basics and use grading to make smarter collecting choices.

Coins are typically graded on a **70-point scale**, with 1 being the lowest (barely recognizable) and 70 being perfect. This is known as the **Sheldon Scale**. A coin's grade depends on several factors, including:

- **Wear**: The amount of detail lost due to circulation
- **Luster**: The coin's natural shine
- **Strike**: How clearly the design was stamped
- **Marks**: Scratches, dings, or contact with other coins

Here are some common grading terms:

- **Poor (P-1)**: The coin is badly worn, and only the outline is visible.
- **Good (G-4)**: Most design elements are flat, but the coin is still identifiable.
- **Very Fine (VF-20 to VF-35)**: Moderate wear with many details visible.
- **Extremely Fine (EF or XF-40 to XF-45)**: Light wear, strong details.
- **About Uncirculated (AU-50 to AU-58)**: Very slight wear, mostly sharp.
- **Mint State (MS-60 to MS-70)**: No wear from circulation. MS-70 is a perfect coin, often seen in proof or slabbed examples.

Mint state coins are further split into subgrades. An MS-63 coin may have minor marks, while an MS-67 is nearly flawless. The higher the number, the more desirable the coin.

Grading takes practice. You can compare your coins to certified examples or use visual grading charts. Over time, your eye will improve, and you'll develop a sense for what makes one coin more valuable than another.

23. Where to Get Error Coins Certified: PCGS, NGC, and ANACS

Once you believe you have a valuable coin, especially a mint error or high-grade example, **certification** becomes important. Certification means sending the coin to a professional grading service. They will authenticate it, assign a grade, and seal it in a tamper-proof holder.

There are three main coin grading services in the United States:

PCGS – Professional Coin Grading Service

Founded in 1986, **PCGS** is one of the most respected grading companies in the world. Coins graded by PCGS are widely trusted and often command higher prices. Their holders are sturdy, and the certification label includes the grade, serial number, and variety if applicable.

PCGS also offers online verification, where you can check the coin's information using its unique ID.

NGC – Numismatic Guaranty Company

NGC is another top-tier grading company, known for consistent and reliable grading. Their holders feature a white background that makes coins easy to view. NGC is especially popular with collectors of modern coins, world coins, and certified bullion.

Like PCGS, NGC allows for variety attribution and offers population reports showing how many coins of a certain grade exist.

ANACS – American Numismatic Association Certification Service

ANACS is the oldest grading service in the United States. While not as prominent as PCGS or NGC, ANACS is well-known for grading **error coins**. Their certification often includes specific error types, such as off-center strikes, cuds, or planchet flaws.

ANACS is also more affordable and has a reputation for quick turnaround times. If your focus is mint errors, they are an excellent choice.

24. Slabbed Coins vs Raw Coins

When a coin is graded by a certification service, it is sealed in a hard plastic holder called a **slab**. This protects the coin and ensures buyers that it has been authenticated. A **slabbed coin** carries more credibility and often a higher market value than an identical **raw coin**, which has not been certified.

Advantages of Slabbed Coins

- **Authentication**: Proven to be genuine
- **Grading**: Assigned an official condition rating
- **Protection**: Encased in durable material that prevents damage
- **Resale value**: Easier to sell and often worth more
- **Tamper-proof**: Sealed and traceable through verification systems

Disadvantages

- **Cost**: Certification fees can be expensive, especially for low-value coins
- **Wait time**: Submitting coins can take weeks
- **Non-reversible**: Removing a coin from a slab voids the grade

Raw Coins

Many collectors still enjoy collecting **raw coins**, especially when building starter sets or focusing on coins found in circulation. While raw coins are cheaper and more accessible, they require careful storage and are more vulnerable to damage, counterfeits, and disputes over grade.

When buying raw coins, use caution. Always deal with trusted sellers, and if a coin looks too good to be true, consider having it authenticated.

25. Alternatives to the PCGS Price Guide

The **PCGS Price Guide** is one of the most popular tools for estimating coin values, but it is not the only option. Knowing where to find up-to-date and reliable pricing information helps collectors make informed buying and selling decisions.

The Red Book

The **Guide Book of United States Coins**, known as the **Red Book**, is a yearly publication that lists retail values for U.S. coins. It is an excellent reference for collectors and includes history, mintage numbers, and average values by grade.

While not always current with market trends, it remains one of the most widely used books in coin collecting.

NGC Price Guide

NGC offers its own online **price guide**, covering both certified and raw coins. Like PCGS, it updates regularly and is integrated with population data and auction history. It is especially helpful for collectors of modern coins and bullion pieces.

Numismedia and Greysheet

Numismedia provides pricing for a wide range of U.S. coins, including dealer market values. It is often used by dealers to track wholesale and retail trends.

Greysheet (published as the Coin Dealer Newsletter) is a subscription-based service used by professionals. It gives current pricing based on actual dealer-to-dealer transactions and is considered a market reality check.

Online Auction Sites

Sites like **eBay**, **Heritage Auctions**, and **GreatCollections** offer real-time pricing based on actual sales. By searching for recent sold listings, you can get a feel for what a coin is really worth in the current market.

26. Proof Set Errors and Uncirculated Mint Set Finds

While proof sets and mint sets are intended to be flawless, they are not immune to mistakes. In fact, many valuable mint errors have come directly from these government-issued coin collections.

Proof Set Errors

Proof coins are specially struck for collectors using polished dies and multiple strikes. They are sold in hard plastic cases and often have a mirror-like finish. Because of their careful production, proof errors are rare but highly collectible when found.

Types of proof errors include:

- **Missing frosting**: Design elements that should be frosted appear shiny.
- **Cameo imbalance**: One side is frosted and the other is not.
- **Misaligned dies**: Proof coins with off-center features.
- **Struck through**: Foreign objects like fibers or grease affect the design.
- **Wrong planchets**: Coins struck on blanks meant for other denominations.

One famous example is the **1970-S proof quarter** struck on a dime planchet. These types of errors are incredibly rare and often found only when collectors break open proof sets.

Mint Set Finds

Uncirculated mint sets are issued each year and include coins from all operating mints. While not struck with the same care as proofs, these coins are often in high grades and make excellent hunting grounds for minor errors.

Common finds in mint sets include:

- **Die cracks** and **chips**
- **Repunched mint marks**
- **Small off-center strikes**
- **Strikethroughs** caused by debris in the die
- **Missing elements**, such as incomplete rims or faint lettering

Mint sets are also useful for comparing coins from different mints side by side.

Sometimes, variations in strike quality or finish can reveal subtle varieties not easily noticed in loose change.

SECTION 6
FAMOUS ERROR COIN CASES

27. The 1913 Liberty Head Nickel

Error coins come in many forms, but a select few stand out as legends. These coins are not just mint mistakes. They are historical artifacts, million-dollar rarities, and icons of American numismatics. Some were created accidentally. Others have mysterious origins. But all have captured the imagination of collectors and investors for decades.

Let's explore the most famous error coins in U.S. history and the stories behind them.

The **1913 Liberty Head nickel** is perhaps the most mysterious and controversial coin in American history. Officially, the U.S. Mint stopped producing Liberty Head nickels in 1912. The design was replaced by the Buffalo nickel in 1913. Yet somehow, five Liberty Head nickels dated 1913 were struck and made their way into private hands.

No official record of their production exists. The most widely accepted theory is that a Mint employee, likely Samuel W. Brown, struck the coins unofficially and later revealed them while working as a coin dealer. By 1920, all five were accounted for and began to trade hands among elite collectors.

The coins are exceptionally rare and valuable. One example, known as the **Olsen specimen**, was even featured on an episode of *Hawaii Five-O* in 1973. Another, the **Walton specimen**, was believed lost for decades until it resurfaced in 2003.

Each of the five nickels is now in a museum or private collection. In recent years, these coins have sold for **up to $5 million** each, making the 1913 Liberty Head nickel one of the most valuable error coins ever.

28. The 1943 Copper Penny

1943 Copper Penny Obverse

During World War II, copper was a vital material used in military manufacturing. To conserve it, the U.S. Mint began striking Lincoln cents using zinc-coated steel planchets in 1943. These **steel cents** are common and easily recognized by their silver appearance.

However, a few copper planchets from 1942 remained in the coin presses by mistake. As a result, a small number of **1943 Lincoln cents were struck in bronze**, the normal copper alloy used before and after the war.

These 1943 copper pennies are extremely rare. Estimates suggest that fewer than **30 genuine examples** exist. Most were found accidentally in circulation, discovered by people who noticed their unusual color compared to the steel cents.

To verify whether a 1943 penny is copper or steel, use a simple magnet test. The genuine copper errors will not stick to a magnet. Weight is another clue. Copper cents weigh about **3.11 grams**, while steel cents weigh slightly less.

One 1943 copper penny sold for **over $1.7 million** in a private transaction. Others have fetched hundreds of thousands depending on condition. These coins remain some of the most desirable mint errors ever produced.

29. The 1955 Doubled Die Lincoln Cent

The **1955 doubled die cent** is arguably the most famous error that made it into wide circulation. The doubling on this coin is bold and unmistakable. The date, LIBERTY, and IN GOD WE TRUST appear strongly doubled, and the error is visible to the naked eye.

The mistake occurred when the working die received a second hub impression that was misaligned. As a result, thousands of coins were struck with a flawed die before the mistake was noticed.

Interestingly, most of the 1955 doubled dies were released during a night shift at the Philadelphia Mint and ended up in cigarette vending machine rolls across the northeastern United States. Collectors were stunned to find these errors in their change, and demand for them grew rapidly.

Estimates suggest that **20,000 to 24,000 examples** were released, though far fewer remain in mint state. Well-circulated examples still sell for several hundred dollars, while uncirculated pieces can bring **$1,500 to $5,000 or more**.

This coin remains one of the best-known examples of a dramatic doubled die and is a must-have for Lincoln cent specialists.

30. The 1972 Doubled Die Lincoln Cent

Seventeen years after the 1955 issue, another striking doubled die emerged. The **1972 doubled die obverse** is bold and dramatic, though it is slightly less famous than its predecessor. The doubling is most evident in the date and the inscriptions LIBERTY and IN GOD WE TRUST.

Unlike the 1955 cent, which has only one major doubled die variety, the 1972 cent has multiple recognized variations. However, **"DDO-001"**, the most dramatic of them all, is the version that commands significant attention and value.

The error was created in a similar way to the 1955 version through a misaligned hubbing process. Because of improved detection and production control by the 1970s, fewer of these errors slipped through. Even so, enough were released that collectors had a chance to find them in circulation.

High-grade examples certified by PCGS or NGC can sell for **$300 to $800**, with the best specimens exceeding **$1,000**. The 1972 doubled die helped renew interest in modern errors and proved that valuable mistakes could still happen even in the era of tighter quality control.

31. Other Notable Error Coin Legends

While the previous examples are well-known among collectors, several other U.S. error coins have achieved legendary status due to their uniqueness, rarity, or dramatic appearance.

1995 Doubled Die Lincoln Cent

The **1995 doubled die cent** was one of the first modern error coins to go viral among collectors. Though the doubling is much more subtle than the 1955 or 1972 examples, it still attracted national attention. The U.S. Mint even acknowledged it, adding to its popularity.

The doubling appears mostly in LIBERTY. While the value is modest, often **$20 to $50** in uncirculated grades, it remains a fan favorite and is commonly found in error coin collections.

2004-D Wisconsin Extra Leaf Quarters

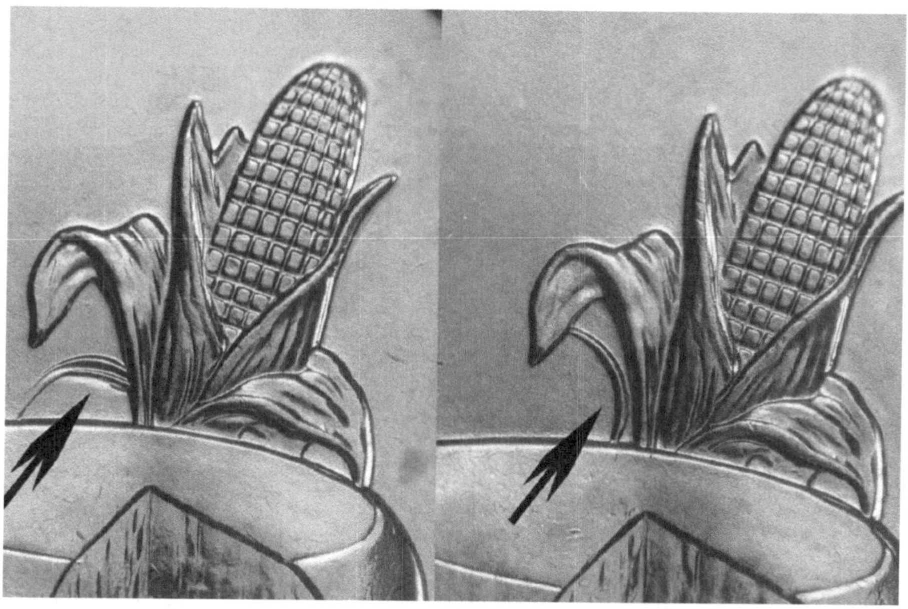

The **2004 Wisconsin quarter** from the State Quarters series gained fame due to an extra leaf that appears on the ear of corn in the reverse design. There are two varieties: the **Extra Leaf High** and the **Extra Leaf Low**. These are believed to be die gouges or polishing errors but were significant enough to be recognized by grading services.

Values range from **$50 to $300 or more**, depending on condition and demand. Their presence in a modern series made them especially appealing to younger collectors and those who hunt through rolls.

2000-P Sacagawea Dollar Mule with Quarter Obverse

Mentioned earlier in this book, the **Sacagawea dollar mule** is among the most valuable mint errors in history. It combines the obverse of a Washington quarter with the reverse of a Sacagawea dollar on a golden-colored dollar planchet. Multiple examples have sold for over **$100,000**, and their rarity has made them one of the most studied errors in U.S. mint history.

1982 No Mint Mark Roosevelt Dime

Most dimes minted in Philadelphia from 1980 onward bear a "P" mint mark. In 1982, however, a small number of dimes were released without any mint mark at all. These **1982 no-P dimes** were true mint errors, not worn coins, and were struck using dies that had skipped the mint mark punching process.

They can sell for **$100 to $300**, especially in high grade. Their discovery helped reinforce the importance of watching even modern coinage closely.

SECTION 7
RARE AND VALUABLE ERROR COINS

32. The Most Valuable Error Coins in US History

Some error coins go beyond curiosity and enter the realm of numismatic legends. These coins are not just collectible, they are among the most coveted items in American coinage history. Their value comes from a combination of extreme rarity, dramatic minting flaws, and historical intrigue.

1955 Doubled Die Lincoln Cent

Perhaps the most famous U.S. error coin, the 1955 doubled die cent was struck when a working die received a second, misaligned impression. The result is unmistakable: doubling of the entire obverse design, especially visible in LIBERTY and IN GOD WE TRUST. These coins were released in regular circulation, making their discovery even more exciting. High-grade examples have sold for tens of thousands of dollars.

2000 Sacagawea Dollar Mule

This astonishing coin was struck with the obverse of a Washington quarter and the reverse of a Sacagawea dollar, using different dies from two denominations. Only a few dozen are known. They first surfaced from coin rolls in vending machine stock and have since sold for as much as $200,000.

1943 Copper Penny

During World War II, the U.S. Mint switched to steel planchets for pennies to save copper for the war effort. However, a few 1943 pennies were accidentally struck on leftover copper planchets. These are among the most valuable error coins ever found, with one example selling for over $1 million.

1969-S Doubled Die Cent

Similar to the 1955 cent, this coin features dramatic doubling on the obverse. Because of its bold visuals and low survival numbers, it is considered one of the "big four" in doubled die errors. Counterfeits are common, so certification is a must.

These top-tier coins set the standard for how valuable error coins can become when extreme rarity meets major visual impact.

33. Evaluating an Error Coin's True Worth

Determining how much a mint error is worth involves several key factors. While some coins may look odd or unique, only specific characteristics add real value. Collectors and dealers alike look for the following elements:

Type of Error

Some error types are inherently more valuable than others. Dramatic, rare errors like mules, double denominations, and major off-center strikes are more prized than minor die cracks or small planchet flaws. Doubled dies and repunched mint marks also hold strong appeal, especially when confirmed and listed in guides.

Visibility and Eye Appeal

Errors that are easily visible without magnification tend to bring higher prices. A bold off-center strike or large cud is easier to recognize and attracts more interest than subtle flaws that require careful examination.

Condition of the Coin

Just like with regular coins, the grade plays a major role in valuation. An error in Mint State condition can be worth many times more than the same error on a heavily worn coin. Preservation adds value.

Rarity and Population

How many of the error type are known to exist? If only a handful are certified, the value increases. Coins that were widely produced but have few known errors from a particular year or mint mark can become hot collector targets.

Certification

Certified coins from PCGS, NGC, or ANACS carry a premium due to guaranteed authenticity and error attribution. Raw coins with errors should be submitted for grading if they appear valuable or unusual.

Always compare your coin to confirmed sales, price guides, and online databases. Auction records are especially helpful for seeing what collectors have recently paid for similar pieces.

34. Auctions, Dealers, and Cherrypickers' Guide Tips

Finding, valuing, and selling error coins is easier with the right resources. Understanding where to buy and sell, and how to identify worthwhile coins, is a major part of the hobby.

Coin Auctions

Auction houses such as Heritage Auctions, Stack's Bowers, and GreatCollections specialize in certified error coins. Their online archives are excellent places to study real-world pricing. Many high-end errors are sold this way, especially those with dramatic appearances or low populations.

Even eBay can be a useful platform, but only if you stick to verified sellers and closely examine listing details and images. Beware of overhyped or misidentified coins.

Coin Dealers

Reputable dealers often have years of experience and may specialize in errors or varieties. They can provide immediate offers or help you understand a coin's potential. However, dealers must also make a profit, so selling directly to them may bring lower payouts than auctioning.

Always check dealer reviews and credentials, and when possible, get multiple opinions before parting with a valuable coin.

The Cherrypickers' Guide

This essential two-volume set is the bible for collectors of errors and varieties. It lists hundreds of known mint errors and includes pictures, values, diagnostics, and historical notes. If you want to learn how to spot rare varieties hiding in common coins, this book is your best companion.

The term "cherrypicking" refers to the act of finding a valuable coin among common examples. With a sharp eye and this guide, you might spot a hundred-dollar error in a five-dollar coin box.

35. Investing in Coins for the Long Term

Mint error coins are not just collectible. They can also be investments. Like fine art or vintage cars, rare coins have a long history of retaining value, and in some cases, increasing significantly over time.

What Makes Errors a Strong Investment?

1. **Rarity**: Limited numbers mean steady demand and rising prices when supply is exhausted.
2. **Eye appeal**: Dramatic errors are visually engaging and remain desirable.
3. **Historical intrigue**: Error coins often come with stories, which adds to their collectible status.
4. **Market visibility**: Well-known errors are widely recognized and easy to resell.

Risk and Patience

As with all investments, patience is required. Not every coin will rise in value quickly. Condition matters, and market demand can fluctuate. You should avoid overpaying during hype periods and focus on coins that have a solid reputation among collectors.

Building a well-rounded portfolio of certified, high-quality error coins is a smart strategy. Avoid coins with limited documentation or that require explanations to justify their value.

Coins with a proven track record, such as the 1955 DDO or 2000 mule dollar, are likely to hold and grow in value. Set a budget, do your research, and think long-term.

36. Making Money with Error Coins

Error coin collecting can actually be a profitable hobby. Many collectors start by searching coin rolls, change jars, or flea markets, looking for overlooked mint mistakes. With time and experience, you can turn small finds into real income.

Roll Searching

Coin roll hunting is a low-cost, high-reward method. Buy rolls of cents, nickels, or dimes from your local bank, then inspect them for errors like off-center strikes, doubling, or missing elements. Replace common coins and keep the valuable ones.

Collectors have found BIE Lincoln cents, 1972 doubled dies, and clipped planchets this way. It takes patience, but you pay only face value.

Buying and Reselling

Another way to profit is to buy undervalued error coins from estate sales, coin shops, or online auctions. If you spot an unrecognized error or find a coin that could benefit from certification, you may be able to flip it for a profit.

Learn to recognize underappreciated varieties. Sometimes sellers miss key diagnostics, and you can use your knowledge to capitalize on their oversight.

Online Selling

Platforms like eBay or Facebook Marketplace allow you to reach collectors directly. A well-described listing with clear photos and authentication can bring strong returns.

To succeed in selling, build a reputation for honesty and accuracy. The more trust you earn in the community, the easier it becomes to move coins at fair prices.

SECTION 8
FUTURE OF ERROR COINS

37. Evolving US Minting Processes and Error Rates

The United States Mint has come a long way since the early 1800s, when coins were produced with hand-operated presses and errors were routine. Today, the minting process is largely automated, and quality control is tighter than ever. Still, mistakes continue to occur, and those few that do are even more desirable because of their rarity.

In the early 20th century, it was not uncommon for off-center strikes, planchet flaws, and misaligned dies to go unnoticed. Presses were manually adjusted, and human involvement increased the likelihood of mistakes.

By contrast, the modern U.S. Mint operates with high-speed robotic systems that can produce hundreds of coins per minute with extreme precision. Coins are now struck on automated presses that include sensors, cameras, and software designed to identify and reject imperfect strikes in real time.

Despite these improvements, no system is perfect. Errors still slip through. In fact, as minting has become faster, certain types of errors have become more frequent again. Examples include die polishing errors, weak strikes, missing edge lettering, and minor planchet defects.

The push for quantity sometimes introduces opportunities for machine-related flaws. With fewer employees physically inspecting coins, some mistakes go undetected during packaging and distribution. This creates an interesting paradox: as technology aims for perfection, rare imperfections may become even more valued by collectors.

38. Technological Advances and How They Change Coin Production

Recent years have seen major technological advancements in coin production, including:

- **Laser engraving** of dies
- **Computerized hubbing and die creation**
- **Optical sorting and vision systems**
- **Advanced alloy testing and material scanning**
- **AI-based inspection algorithms**

These upgrades make it easier for the Mint to maintain consistent quality. For example, die creation now involves digital scanning, removing much of the risk once associated with manual die hubbing. As a result, errors like the famous doubled die of 1955 are nearly impossible to reproduce today.

Edge lettering, which used to be applied by an additional machine, is now incorporated into some presses directly. This helps prevent missing or upside-down lettering, which previously led to error coins on Presidential dollars and other series.

The use of automated vision systems means thousands of coins can be checked per hour. These systems are programmed to detect deviations in design, color, and reflectivity. Still, they are not flawless. Human error during programming, mechanical wear, or miscalibration can allow a small number of flawed coins to pass through.

While older errors like clipped planchets or off-center strikes have become rarer, modern errors include:

- **Struck-through grease or debris**
- **Edge lettering anomalies**
- **Laser burn-throughs or incomplete frosting on proofs**
- **Intentional experimental issues** like satin finishes or enhanced strikes

Collectors must now learn to recognize new types of errors specific to high-tech production, requiring updated reference guides and deeper study of minting techniques.

39. Predictions: Which Errors Will Increase in Value?

Looking ahead, which error coins are likely to appreciate in the coming years? While no one can predict the market with certainty, there are key indicators that suggest which coins have strong long-term potential.

1. Dramatic Visual Errors

Coins with bold, visible mistakes, such as large off-center strikes, missing designs, or doubled elements, continue to hold collector interest. These errors are instantly recognizable and often appeal to beginners and seasoned numismatists alike.

As fewer dramatic errors are made, older examples in high grade will likely rise in value. Think of coins like the 1972 doubled die cent or the 2004 Wisconsin quarter with the extra leaf. These are easy to explain, easy to spot, and still rare enough to generate demand.

2. Errors from Limited-Issue Coins

Mint products with low mintage numbers, such as special collector editions or low-run bullion coins, have a smaller chance of producing error coins. When errors do occur in these limited runs, they can command very high premiums.

Examples include:

- Proof Silver Eagles with missing frosting
- Burnished coins struck with wrong dies
- Coins struck on wrong planchets during transition years

As collectors chase completeness, an error variety from a rare series may become the missing piece for many sets.

3. Modern Errors with Strong Certification

Third-party certification has made modern errors more credible. Coins with official error designations from PCGS, NGC, or ANACS, especially those in mint state, have a better chance of increasing in value over time.

Buyers trust certified errors more than raw coins. A coin labeled “off-center strike 10 percent” or “double denomination error” with a numerical grade offers confidence and standardization.

4. Transitional Errors

Coins struck during design or metal composition changes have historical significance. Examples include the 1965 silver transition coins or the 1982 copper-zinc Lincoln cent mix-ups. As future transitions occur, such as potential changes in coin alloys or mint locations, new transitional errors may emerge and gain value quickly.

5. Errors from New Series

Every new coin series offers the chance for new errors. When the State Quarters launched, no one expected the rise of errors like the Wisconsin leaf variety. Future releases, such as the American Women Quarters or new dollar coins, may produce fresh, collectable mistakes.

Collectors who pay attention early can often acquire these varieties before they hit mainstream awareness.

40. How the Numismatic Journal Shapes Market Trends

Publications like the **Numismatic Journal**, **Coin World**, and **The Numismatist** play a vital role in shaping collector focus, market value, and industry knowledge. These journals act as both educators and influencers, spotlighting new discoveries, historical insights, and auction results.

Why These Journals Matter

- **Error Discovery**: Many modern error coins first gain attention through journal features or reader submissions. Collectors regularly send photos and reports of unusual finds, which sometimes lead to major discoveries.
- **Market Signals**: Articles on price increases, demand shifts, or new grading standards can influence what collectors pursue. When a well-known publication highlights an error coin or variety, interest usually follows.
- **Educational Content**: Journals help clarify what qualifies as a mint error versus post-mint damage. This guidance helps prevent misunderstandings and protects collectors from scams or overpriced coins.
- **Expert Interviews and Case Studies**: Conversations with Mint employees, auctioneers, and grading experts provide insider views that are not available elsewhere. This kind of insight shapes future collecting strategies.
- **Trend Forecasting**: Publications often publish annual predictions about what to watch in the coming year. Topics include upcoming coin programs, low mintage alerts, and speculation on series that may contain profitable varieties.

Digital Reach and Online Extensions

In the past, only monthly printed journals existed. Today, these publications have extended into digital platforms. Blogs, podcasts, webinars, and collector forums expand the reach of numismatic education. Social media allows for immediate feedback and discussion, creating a global network of collectors who influence each other in real time.

Being plugged into these communities allows collectors to stay ahead of the curve. When new errors surface or auction records are broken, you are more likely to hear about it first through these outlets.

The future of error coin collecting is not fading but merely evolving. As minting technology improves and the U.S. Mint continues to innovate, the types of errors collectors chase may shift, but the excitement will remain.

From transitional errors and advanced die flaws to edge lettering problems and new reverse designs, the hobby continues to reward those who stay curious, informed, and attentive to detail.

Publications like the Numismatic Journal and modern certification standards give collectors powerful tools. And as coins become more precise, the few mistakes that do emerge will become even more valuable.

Whether you are drawn to old-school classics like the 1955 doubled die or the sharp precision of a modern Silver Eagle struck with a frost flaw, one thing is clear. The world of error coins has a bright future, and now is a great time to be part of it.

SECTION 9
BUYING, SELLING, AND SPOTTING FAKES

41. Tips for Buying Error Coins from Dealers or Auctions

Buying error coins can be one of the most exciting and rewarding parts of the hobby. Whether you're looking for a dramatic off-center strike or a rare doubled die, making smart purchasing decisions ensures you're getting what you pay for and building a high-quality collection.

Buy Certified When Possible

The safest way to buy error coins is to purchase examples that have been certified by a reputable grading service like **PCGS**, **NGC**, or **ANACS**. These services not only grade the coin's condition but also verify the type of error. You'll receive the coin in a secure holder with a clear label describing the error and grade.

Certified coins may cost more, but they reduce the risk of buying fakes or misidentified items. They are also easier to resell, as most buyers prefer slabbed coins for security and confidence.

Understand the Market

Before making a purchase, research the specific error you're targeting. Check auction results, collector forums, and recent sales listings to understand current pricing. Look at coins in similar condition with the same error type and determine whether the coin you're considering is priced fairly.

Use multiple sources like the **Cherrypickers' Guide**, **PCGS Price Guide**, and actual sold listings on eBay and GreatCollections to confirm your understanding of the coin's value.

Ask Questions

When buying from a dealer or auction, never hesitate to ask for additional information. A reputable seller should be willing to provide high-quality images, describe the coin in detail, and answer questions about the origin, grading history, or authenticity. If a seller avoids direct answers or pressures you to act quickly, that is a red flag.

Choose the Right Auction Venue

There are many ways to buy coins at auction on online platforms like eBay, major auction houses like Heritage, or even local coin shows. Stick to reputable auction houses for high-value purchases, as they often screen consignments and stand behind their descriptions.

For eBay and other user-based sites, check the seller's feedback, read listings carefully, and confirm that the photos match the description.

42. Warning Signs of Fake or Misrepresented Errors

The world of error coin collecting is filled with legitimate finds, but also with misleading listings, altered coins, and outright counterfeits. Knowing how to recognize these warning signs is essential to avoid disappointment or financial loss.

Post-Mint Damage Passed Off as Errors

One of the most common mistakes new collectors make is buying coins that look odd but are not true mint errors. Examples include:

- Coins that are bent, scratched, or smashed intentionally
- Coins with holes, cuts, or marks added after minting
- "Hammered" coins that appear double struck but were manually altered

These types of damage are sometimes sold as "errors" by dishonest sellers. If the flaw could have happened outside the mint, it likely holds no added value.

Always remember: **a real mint error must have occurred during the minting process**, not after the coin left the facility.

Suspicious Doubling

Many listings show coins with minor doubling on the date or letters and call them "doubled dies." In reality, most are just **machine doubling**, a flattening caused by a loose die during striking. Unlike true doubled die coins, machine doubling does not raise the profile of the design. It looks shelf-like, flat, and lacks clear separation between doubled features.

If you're unsure whether the doubling is real, compare it with confirmed examples from a trusted source. Online references and certified coin images are excellent comparison tools.

Too Good to Be True

If a coin seems extremely rare, but the price is low and the seller has limited background, approach with caution. Rare mint errors, especially dramatic or high-grade ones, are well-known in the hobby and rarely appear undervalued unless there is a catch.

Avoid listings that:

- Lack clear, close-up images
- Provide no details about the error or variety

- Use generic titles like “must-see error” or “unbelievable find” without specifics

Watch for Altered Coins

Some coins are altered to mimic known errors. For instance:

- Two coins are fused together to look like a double denomination
- A quarter design is carved onto a Sacagawea dollar to imitate a mule error
- Surfaces are manipulated to fake a lamination peel

These types of counterfeits can be very convincing to untrained eyes. Always check the weight, metal composition, and design alignment of any suspicious piece. Use a digital scale, magnet, and comparison images when available.

If you suspect a coin may be fake, do not buy it unless it has been authenticated by a major grading service.

43. Selling Your Error Coins Online or Locally

Selling your error coins can be just as enjoyable as collecting them. Whether you are upgrading your collection, downsizing, or trying to profit from your finds, knowing where and how to sell makes a big difference.

Know Your Coin's Value

Before listing or offering your coin to anyone, make sure you understand its market value. Check recent sales for similar items, especially ones in comparable condition. Price guides can give you a rough estimate, but **real-world sales data** is often more useful.

If your coin is certified, include the certification number in your research to see what similar coins with the same grade and error type have sold for recently.

Sell to the Right Audience

Depending on your coin, the best buyer may vary. Here are common options:

- **Online marketplaces** like eBay allow you to reach collectors directly, but require time and strong presentation.
- **Coin shows** offer a fast way to sell in person. Dealers may pay less, but there is no shipping or listing involved.
- **Auction houses** like Heritage or GreatCollections are excellent for rare, high-end errors. They charge fees, but also handle marketing and buyer screening.
- **Local coin shops** are convenient and can offer instant cash. However, expect a wholesale price.

If your coin has a broader appeal, such as a dramatic error or something listed in the Cherrypickers' Guide, it is worth promoting to the wider collector market.

Present Your Coin Professionally

The better your coin looks online or in person, the better your chances of a strong sale. Include:

- Clear, high-resolution photos (front and back, with close-ups of the error)
- A full description of the coin's details, including date, mint mark, grade (if known), and error type
- The certification number if the coin is slabbed
- Honest condition notes: do not oversell or hide flaws

Buyers appreciate transparency. Being accurate builds trust and leads to positive feedback or repeat business.

Protect Yourself as a Seller

When shipping coins:

- Use protective packaging and secure envelopes or boxes
- Include tracking and insurance for valuable items
- Never tape coins directly or send them loose in the package

Keep copies of all communication and transactions. If you're selling online, use platforms with buyer and seller protections to reduce risk.

Consider Timing

Some coins sell better at certain times. Tax refund season, national coin shows, and right after a major numismatic event can all bring more traffic. Stay active in collector forums and groups to catch trends and take advantage of spikes in interest.

44. Coin Appraisal Services You Can Trust

When you find a coin that looks valuable or unusual, getting it professionally appraised is the best way to understand its true worth. A coin appraisal determines a coin's market value based on condition, rarity, demand, and, in the case of error coins, the type and visibility of the mint mistake. But not all appraisal services are created equal.

Start by choosing an appraisal from a **reputable dealer or professional coin grading service**. Trusted grading companies like **PCGS (Professional Coin Grading Service)**, **NGC (Numismatic Guaranty Company)**, and **ANACS (American Numismatic Association Certification Service)** not only grade coins but often offer appraisal services or recommended partners.

If your coin is uncertified, these companies can also provide authentication, assign a grade, and formally document any error or variety it contains. Once slabbed and labeled, a coin's value becomes easier to verify and more trusted by collectors and buyers.

Local coin shops can also provide appraisals. Choose dealers who are members of respected organizations such as the **American Numismatic Association (ANA)** or the **Professional Numismatists Guild (PNG)**. Ask for their credentials, how they evaluate coins, and whether they charge an appraisal fee.

For high-value coins, consider getting multiple opinions. Comparing appraisals from different sources gives you a better idea of the true market value and helps you avoid underpricing or overestimating your coin's worth.

45. Understanding Market Trends in 2025

As of 2025, the coin market continues to evolve. Several trends are influencing how error coins are bought, sold, and valued.

First, **modern errors are gaining popularity**. Collectors who used to focus on older coins are now seeking dramatic mistakes from recent mint issues, such as misaligned dies, missing edge lettering, and struck-through coins from popular series like the American Women Quarters or Silver Eagles.

Second, **online auctions have become the dominant way to track and influence coin prices**. Sites like eBay, GreatCollections, and Heritage Auctions provide real-time data, helping collectors understand what coins are actually selling for, not just what price guides suggest.

Third, **certified coins continue to outperform raw coins**. Buyers prefer PCGS- or NGC-graded error coins, especially when the error is clearly labeled on the holder. As a result, uncertified coins, even if authentic, often sell for less.

Lastly, **demand remains strong for dramatic visual errors** and coins listed in reference books like the Cherrypickers' Guide. As younger collectors enter the hobby, clear visuals and strong narratives are driving purchases.

To stay ahead, follow auction results, read collector blogs, and watch what seasoned dealers are buying. The more you understand the market, the better your collecting and selling decisions will be.

CONCLUSION AND REFERENCE

46. Error Coin Encyclopedia: Quick Reference Sheet

This compact guide lists some of the most important terms, error types, and indicators to help you spot, understand, and describe mint errors.

Common Error Types

Doubled Die

Design elements, especially letters or numbers, appear duplicated due to a misalignment in the die creation process.

Off-Center Strike

A coin that is struck when the planchet is not properly centered between the dies, leaving part of the design missing.

Clipped Planchet

The coin appears to have a curved or straight section missing from its edge, caused by overlapping punches during blanking.

Broadstrike

A coin struck without the retaining collar, resulting in an expanded, rimless appearance.

Lamination Error

Caused by a flaw in the metal alloy. It results in peeling or cracked surfaces.

Die Crack

Raised lines on the coin where the die cracked during use.

Cud

A raised blob of metal on the edge of a coin caused by a piece of the die breaking off.

Struck Through

Foreign material (like grease, wire, or cloth) gets between the die and planchet, leaving an impression or void.

Mule Error

A coin struck with mismatched dies from different coin types or denominations.

Repunched Mint Mark (RPM)

A mint mark that appears doubled or shadowed due to being punched more than once in slightly different positions.

Rotated Die

The reverse side of the coin is misaligned when flipped vertically.

Wrong Planchet

A coin struck on a planchet intended for a different denomination.

Helpful Tools

- **5x–10x Magnifier or Loupe**
- **Digital Scale (grams)**
- **Calipers or ruler**
- **The Cherrypickers' Guide**
- **Online auction archives and coin forums**
- **PCGS or NGC population reports and price guides**

47. Top 20 Error Coins You Can Still Find in Circulation

Here are twenty valuable or highly collectible U.S. error coins that still occasionally appear in circulation, coin rolls, or inherited collections.

1. 1995 Doubled Die Obverse Lincoln Cent

Look for strong doubling in LIBERTY and IN GOD WE TRUST.

2. 1972 Doubled Die Obverse Lincoln Cent

One of the most dramatic doubled dies in circulation.

3. 1983 Doubled Die Reverse Lincoln Cent

Rare but still found in circulation with careful searching.

4. 1982 Small Date Copper Cent

Copper (3.11g) version is rare; most were zinc (2.5g).

5. 1992 Close AM Lincoln Cent

The spacing between the A and M in AMERICA is abnormally tight.

6. 1999 Wide AM Lincoln Cent

Opposite of the 1992 error. Designed for proof coins but used on circulation strikes.

7. 1982 No Mint Mark Roosevelt Dime

Only found from Philadelphia, where mint marks were normally reintroduced.

8. 2004-D Wisconsin Quarter "Extra Leaf"

Two varieties exist: Low Leaf and High Leaf. Highly sought after.

9. 2005 Kansas Quarter "In God We Rust"

Die grease error that removes the T in TRUST.

10. 2000-P Sacagawea Dollar / State Quarter Mule

Extremely rare, but worth noting as it has appeared in circulation.

11. 1965–1967 Silver Error Coins

Look for silver coins mistakenly struck in years after silver was removed.

12. 1970-S Small Date Lincoln Cent

A proof coin known to have RPMs and other valuable features.

13. 1943 Bronze Lincoln Cent

Though exceedingly rare, a few were released. Most 1943 cents are steel.

14. 1955 Doubled Die Lincoln Cent

Rare in good condition, but fakes abound. Certified examples recommended.

15. 1974-D Aluminum Cent (Experimental)

Only a handful known, but worth knowing about for rare finds.

16. 1989 Wide AM Lincoln Cent (Reverse of 1990)

A transitional variety, extremely hard to find.

17. 1988 Reverse of 1989 Cent

A design change that made its way into circulation.

18. 1998–2000 Close AM Proof Reverse Cents

These were transitional dies that ended up in the wrong production runs.

19. 2001-D Lincoln Cent with Misaligned Die

Subtle, but a good example of how alignment errors work.

20. 2021 Washington Crossing Delaware Quarter Errors

Look for die chips, strikethroughs, and other recent production issues.

Final Encouragement

Keep a small notebook or digital log of your finds. We recommend storing unusual coins in 2x2 holders or flips and labeling them with date, mint mark, error type, and source (change, roll, etc.). The more organized you are, the easier it will be to track value over time and identify patterns.

Error coin collecting is not only about value but also perspective. It teaches patience, trains the eye, and connects you to a deeper appreciation of how even national systems like the U.S. Mint remain, at their core, imperfectly human. Each mistake is a story. And every time you check your change, you are part of the search.

48. Glossary of Coin Terms

Here are some essential terms every coin collector should know, especially when collecting error coins:

Planchet – A blank metal disc that becomes a coin after being struck by dies.

Die – A metal stamp used to impress the design onto a coin.

Mint Mark – A letter indicating where the coin was made (e.g., P for Philadelphia, D for Denver).

Doubled Die – An error caused when a die is impressed twice with a misalignment, resulting in doubled features.

Off-Center Strike – A coin struck when not properly centered, leaving part of the design missing.

Cud – A raised blob of metal on a coin caused by a die break near the rim.

Broadstrike – A coin struck without the retaining collar, causing it to spread and lack a defined rim.

Repunched Mint Mark (RPM) – A mint mark punched more than once in slightly different positions.

Lamination Error – A flaw in the metal that causes peeling or cracks.

Struck Through – An error caused when a coin is struck with debris (like grease or cloth) between the die and the planchet.

Proof Coin – A specially struck coin with high detail and a mirror-like finish, not meant for circulation.

MS (Mint State) – A grading term for uncirculated coins, typically ranging from MS-60 to MS-70.

49. State Quarter Error Checklist

Look for these notable errors in the 50 State Quarters series:

- **2004-D Wisconsin "Extra Leaf High/Low"**
- **2005 Kansas "In God We Rust"**
- **2005 Minnesota "Extra Tree"**
- **2001-P New York "Off-Center Strike"**
- **2000-P South Carolina "Die Crack on Tree"**

Check for missing clad layers, die chips, rotated dies, and doubling. These errors can often be found in circulation or roll searches and remain valuable to collectors.

50. Final Thoughts on the Coin Collecting Hobby

Coin collecting is more than a hobby. It is a pursuit of history, mystery, and sometimes even profit. For collectors of mint errors, the journey is especially rich with surprise and excitement. You're not just assembling coins; you're uncovering the stories they carry and the mistakes that made them stand out from the billions of ordinary pieces that pass through our hands.

The beauty of error coin collecting lies in its accessibility. You do not need to be wealthy to begin. You do not need a museum-grade setup. All it takes is a sharp eye, a bit of curiosity, and the willingness to look more closely at what others ignore. A single doubled die cent found in change or a clipped planchet from a bank roll can be the beginning of a lifelong passion, or a gateway to understanding the incredible precision and occasional chaos of the minting process.

Throughout this book, we have explored the most famous error coins in U.S. history, the different types of mint mistakes, and the grading systems and certification processes that help collectors determine value. We've also looked into the psychology behind collecting, the evolution of the hobby, and the trends influencing the modern coin market. Now, as we conclude, it's worth repeating a simple truth: error coin collecting rewards both patience and knowledge. The more you learn, the better your chances of spotting something rare, and the more meaningful each discovery becomes.

Whether you collect for joy, for investment, or for education, you are joining a community of people who appreciate history in the palm of a hand. Every nick, every off-center strike, every doubled digit tells a story. And in this hobby, those stories are yours to find.

Get Your Free E-book

Get Your Free E-book
Scan the QR code below to instantly access the e-book
'The History of Coin Minting Errors', absolutely free

SCAN ME

https://bonus.grapevinebooks.com/history-of-coin-minting-errors